C.1

j598.13 Blassingame, Wyatt
B
Wonders of the
turtle world

DATE		
JUL 19 1977	NOV 3 1	JUN 1 9 1997
MAY 1 0 1978		AUG 1 2 1997
	JAN	SEP 0 1 1998
JUN 1979	MAY 0 8 1990	FEB 2 3 1999
AUG 1 1 1986		SEP 2 8 1999
JUL 2 1 198	SEP 2 6 1991	
MAY 0 4 1982	AUG 1992	
MAY 3 1 1983	MAR 3 0 1993	
NOV 0 3 1987	DEC 3 0 1993	
	JAN	
OCT 0 4 1989	APR 1 3 1995	

DODD, MEAD WONDERS BOOKS

WONDERS OF ALLIGATORS AND CROCODILES by Wyatt Blassingame
WONDERS OF ANIMAL ARCHITECTURE by Sigmund A. Lavine
WONDERS OF ANIMAL NURSERIES by Jacquelyn Berrill
WONDERS OF BARNACLES by Arnold Ross and William K. Emerson
WONDERS OF THE BAT WORLD by Sigmund A. Lavine
WONDERS BEYOND THE SOLAR SYSTEM by Rocco Feravolo
WONDERS OF THE BISON WORLD by Sigmund A. Lavine and Vincent Scuro
WONDERS OF THE CACTUS WORLD by Sigmund A. Lavine
WONDERS OF CARIBOU by Jim Rearden
WONDERS OF THE DINOSAUR WORLD by William H. Matthews III
WONDERS OF THE EAGLE WORLD by Sigmund A. Lavine
WONDERS OF THE FLY WORLD by Sigmund A. Lavine
WONDERS OF FROGS AND TOADS by Wyatt Blassingame
WONDERS OF GEESE AND SWANS by Thomas D. Fegely
WONDERS OF GEMS by Richard M. Pearl
WONDERS OF GRAVITY by Rocco Feravolo
WONDERS OF THE HAWK WORLD by Sigmund A. Lavine
WONDERS OF HERBS by Sigmund A. Lavine
WONDERS OF HUMMINGBIRDS by Hilda Simon
WONDERS OF THE KELP FOREST by Joseph E. Brown
WONDERS OF MATHEMATICS by Rocco Feravolo
WONDERS OF MEASUREMENT by Owen S. Lieberg
WONDERS OF THE MONKEY WORLD by Jacquelyn Berrill
WONDERS OF THE MOSQUITO WORLD by Phil Ault
WONDERS OF THE OWL WORLD by Sigmund A. Lavine
WONDERS OF THE PELICAN WORLD by Joseph J. Cook and Ralph W. Schreiber
WONDERS OF PRAIRIE DOGS by G. Earl Chace
WONDERS OF ROCKS AND MINERALS by Richard M. Pearl
WONDERS OF SAND by Christie McFall
WONDERS OF SEA GULLS by Elizabeth Anne and Ralph W. Schreiber
WONDERS OF SEALS AND SEA LIONS by Joseph E. Brown
WONDERS OF SOUND by Rocco Feravolo
WONDERS OF THE SPIDER WORLD by Sigmund A. Lavine
WONDERS OF SPONGES by Morris K. Jacobson and Rosemary K. Pang
WONDERS OF STONES by Christie McFall
WONDERS OF THE TREE WORLD by Margaret Cosgrove
WONDERS OF THE TURTLE WORLD by Wyatt Blassingame
WONDERS OF WILD DUCKS by Thomas D. Fegely
WONDERS OF THE WOODS AND DESERT AT NIGHT by Jacquelyn Berrill
WONDERS OF THE WORLD OF THE ALBATROSS by Harvey I. and
    Mildred L. Fisher
WONDERS OF THE WORLD OF BEARS by Bernadine Bailey
WONDERS OF THE WORLD OF HORSES by Sigmund A. Lavine and Brigid Casey
WONDERS OF THE WORLD OF SHELLS by Morris K. Jacobson and
    William K. Emerson
WONDERS OF THE WORLD OF WOLVES by Jacquelyn Berrill
WONDERS OF YOUR SENSES by Margaret Cosgrove

Wonders of the Turtle World

WYATT BLASSINGAME

Illustrated with photographs

DODD, MEAD & COMPANY · NEW YORK

For WYATT LANE
who was much faster than any turtle —
even when on all fours

Photograph Credits

Florida Game & Fresh Water Fish Commission, frontispiece, 8, 10, 11, 17, 52, 55, 57, 60, 68 (bottom), 70; Robert Lane, Silver Springs, Florida, 15, 16, 29; Dave Norris, 51, 68 (top); Dr. Peter C. H. Pritchard, 20, 22, 24, 25, 27, 34, 40, 41, 44, 45, 46, 49, 65, 66, 71, 74, 75; U. S. Fish & Wildlife Service, 61.

Frontispiece: Box turtle, *Terrapene carolina major*

Library of Congress Cataloging in Publication Data

Blassingame, Wyatt.
    Wonders of the turtle world.

    Includes index.
    SUMMARY: Discusses the characteristics and
habits of various species of turtles.
      1. Turtles—Juvenile literature. [1. Turtles]
I. Title.
QL666.C5B55   598.1'3   76–14883
ISBN 0–396–07342–5

Author's Note

I want to thank Dr. Peter C. H. Pritchard, Florida Audubon Society, and Dr. Archie Carr, University of Florida, for their help. From Dr. Carr's superb biography of the green turtle, *So Excellent a Fishe*, I have borrowed much of my information on sea turtles. From Dr. Pritchard's finely detailed *Living Turtles of the World* I have borrowed for both sea and land species. Both gentlemen have patiently answered questions, and tried to point me in the right direction for other answers. Together they are responsible for much of my information, but for none of my mistakes.

Contents

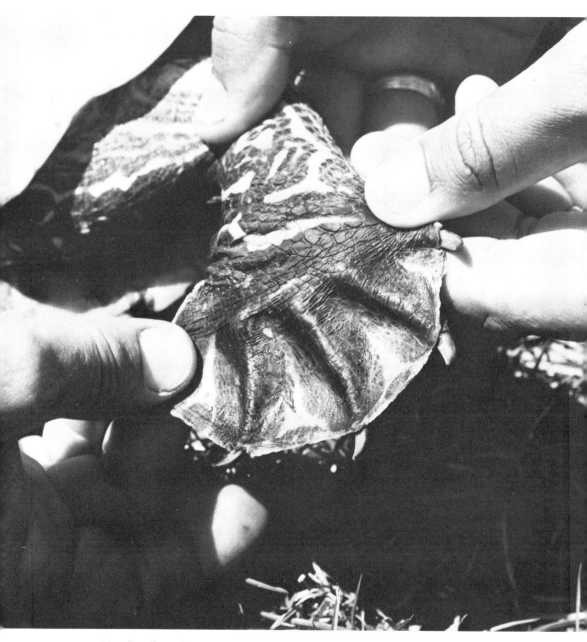

Nearly all freshwater turtles have webbed toes for swimming, and claws for digging when necessary.

I. Turtles, Then and Now

Turtles were among the first animals to crawl out of the sea and take up life on dry land.

When the first dinosaurs appeared on earth, turtles were already here. Wearing their armor of shell, turtles were plodding through forests of strange grasses and giant ferns. And when the dinosaurs disappeared, the turtles stayed on. Later, some of them went back to live in the sea as their ancestors had done. Others stayed on land, looking very much like their descendants look today.

WHAT IS A TURTLE?

The chances are that if you saw a turtle—any kind of turtle, anywhere in the world—you'd know it was a turtle. It would just naturally look like a turtle. But how would you describe turtles in general?

You couldn't do it by size. There are fully grown turtles only a few inches in length, and there are turtles that measure almost eleven feet from the tip of one front flipper to the tip of the other.

Some turtles have legs that look like the stumps of small trees. Some have legs that look like boat paddles.

There are turtles that spend their lives on land. And there are turtles that spend most of their lives at sea.

Probably the shell is the best place to start in describing turtles, since all turtles have shells. But with some this shell is

All turtles have shells, but they vary considerably from species to species. Top: *sawback turtle.* Bottom: *Suwannee River turtle.*

like a big rock, and with some it is more like old leather.

Scientifically, a turtle is a reptile. And a reptile is an animal of which five basic things are true: It has a backbone; it breathes air, not water; it lays eggs that have shells; it has some sort of scales; and it's cold-blooded. (Actually, a reptile's blood isn't really cold. "Cold-blooded" means that the animal has no way of heating its own blood, as does a human being. So its temperature is always the same, or close to the same, as the air or water around it.)

A turtle, then, belongs to the reptile family. But so do snakes, lizards, and alligators.

The thing that makes a turtle a turtle is its shell. And the turtle's shell is actually its skeleton. The turtle has, somehow, managed to grow most of this skeleton on the outside of its body, rather than inside.

This picture of a gopher turtle shows how the carapace and plastron are joined by a bridge at the sides, leaving the front and back open for the head and legs.

Although the shells vary from one species of turtle to another, they are basically the same. There is a top part, called the *carapace*, and a bottom, called the *plastron*. Usually these are joined together on both sides by a bridge of bone. Both the carapace and the plastron are made of two layers. The inner layer of tightly joined bones is the thickest. The outer layer is made of a thin hornlike material, and this is what forms the turtle's scales.

TURTLES, TORTOISES, AND TERRAPINS

Today there are about two hundred different species of turtles. Herpetologists—the people who study turtles and other reptiles—have a scientific name for each species. There is also a common name for each one. In fact, there may be four or five or even more common names for a single species.

To make matters worse, even the word "turtle" may have a different meaning in different parts of the world. In England "turtle" usually means a saltwater turtle, and nothing else. A land turtle is often called a "tortoise," and a freshwater turtle may be called a "terrapin." But "tortoiseshell" jewelry comes from the shell of a seagoing turtle. *"Terrapene"* is part of the scientific name of a land-living box turtle. And the gopher turtle lives in a hole in the ground, not in the sea.

Even the scientists sometimes get mixed up. *Chelonia* is the scientific name for the green turtle. But some use this as a name for all turtles. Others use the name *Testudinata*. Most people, however, will settle for the word "turtle" to cover the whole business. That's how it will be used in this book.

Herpetologists divide turtles into two major groups by the way they hide their heads under their shells. If the turtle bends its neck in an S-shaped curve, as you might push a springy piece of wire into a box, it's a Cryptodira, meaning "hidden neck." Cryptodira are found in North and South America,

12

Europe, Asia, and Africa, just about everywhere turtles are found. If the turtle bends its neck sideways, laying its head alongside its body under the rim of the shell, it's a Pleurodira, a side-necked turtle. These are found only south of the equator, in Africa, South America, and Australia.

We'll take a look at some of the individual species later. First let's consider some of the problems and benefits all turtles have in common.

How turtles breathe

Since the turtle is cold-blooded, it does not burn oxygen from the air for warmth. Therefore it does not need as much air for breathing as does a warm-blooded animal. Even so, it must breathe. But with its ribs grown into a rigid shell, they can't be moved to help with breathing. Instead, the turtle uses a set of muscles close to its back legs. When these contract they pull the turtle's *viscera*—its internal organs—closer together. This causes a partial vacuum that sucks air in through the nose to the lungs. Then the turtle contracts another set of muscles. These push the viscera upward, and force the air out again.

Some water turtles have an extra way of getting oxygen. They take water in through the mouth and pump it across membranes that are somewhat like the gills of a fish. In this way a turtle that's just lying still may live underwater for days. But if the turtle starts to move around, using more air, it will have to come to the surface to breathe

Do turtles live forever?

The truth is, nobody really knows just how long a healthy turtle might live under the proper conditions. One thing is certain, however: it would be a good, long time. Some species live longer than others; but the chances are that a large turtle, kept under perfect conditions, would outlive its human keeper.

Just about the time of the American Revolution, Captain James Cook, a British explorer, took two huge turtles from the Galápagos Islands to the island of Tonga in the South Pacific. Here one of them died just a little over a hundred years later. The other, however, lived until 1966. This would be 190 years in captivity, for a turtle that was fully grown when captured.

At least that's the story. It may possibly be true. On the other hand, many historians believe these turtles were brought to Tonga long after Captain Cook's voyage.

Another Galápagos Islands turtle has become even more famous. After his defeat by the British, Napoleon was sent to prison on the island of Saint Helena. There one of his few pleasures was gardening.

Sir Hudson Lowe, Napoleon's British jailor, had a very twisted sense of humor. He sent to the Galápagos Islands for two giant turtles, and turned them loose in Napoleon's garden. Any big turtle is a natural born bulldozer, and these bulldozed Napoleon's garden into bare land.

Sometime after Napoleon's death in 1821 one of these turtles died. But the other, named Jonathan, is said to be still alive. And not long ago a turtle-fancier in New York asked the history department of a large university to send him to Saint Helena. He had learned turtle-talk, the man said, and he wanted to interview Jonathan—the only living creature that had ever seen Napoleon.

The only thing wrong with this story—aside from the "turtle-talk" being meant as a joke—is that many historians don't agree. Some say Jonathan did not come to Saint Helena until after Napoleon's death.

Either way, Jonathan was—and may still be—a very old turtle indeed.

Probably the large, slow, land turtles, such as those from the Galápagos Islands, live longer than the smaller ones. But even

A number of museums and exhibits now have living Galápagos turtles. And so, eventually, we should know more about just how long they do live. These two turtles are fairly young and small, weighing only about 150 pounds each.

the little box turtle that never gets more than seven inches long is said to have lived for 123 years in captivity. As with Jonathan, there was no one around at the end of that time who had been there in the beginning. So no one could guarantee it was the same turtle.

There is an old belief that you can tell the age of a turtle by counting the "growth rings" on one of its *laminae*. (The laminae are the thin, bony "scales" on the top of its shell.) And it is true that in temperate areas such as the United States these usually form one each year, somewhat like the rings in a tree trunk. However, some turtles have as many as three growth rings when they break out of the egg. And as the turtle gets older, the early rings tend to disappear. This is particularly true where the turtle has a comparatively soft shell. Also, in tropical climates the turtle may continue to grow throughout the years without forming a ring. The little box turtle, however, hibernates in the winter and grows in the summer. So it may have fairly distinct growth rings. And on the box turtle's hard shell these remain visible for a long time. Even so, if the box turtle is more than fifteen years old, the early rings start to disappear.

Most herpetologists now believe that most turtles can live at least thirty or forty years, and possibly much longer. In fact, some scientists believe the turtle may live longer than any other backboned animal on earth, including man.

TURTLE SENSE AND SENSES

Turtles are probably the smartest of all reptiles. But then most reptiles aren't very smart. They can, however, learn the things they truly need to know.

As with most animals, including human beings, turtles learn fastest where food is concerned. In Tallahassee, Florida, Mr. and

Common box turtles. In areas such as northern Florida, where several species of box turtles live close together, they may crossbreed. As a result, although they all look much alike, the markings may vary.

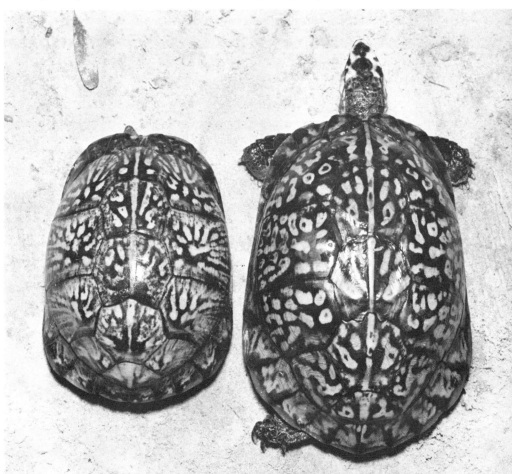

Mrs. Chase Crawford raise turtles for study. If their turtles are fed at the same time and place each day, the turtles quickly learn the time and place. Also, Mrs. Crawford often picks one up to chuck it under the chin. "They like to be petted as much as a dog or cat does," she says.

(The turtles the Crawfords raise are mostly small, good-natured box turtles. Nobody wants to try chucking one of the big snapping turtles under the chin—not unless he wants to lose a finger. More about that in the chapter on snapping turtles.)

The Crawfords keep about eighteen turtles in each pen. Living together, these set up a kind of social order. One becomes the recognized boss and the others keep out of its way. Others may fight—by bumping and pushing—for the best place to sleep, or a particular spot at the feeding pan. But they soon learn which one is strongest, and the fighting stops.

One scientist built a simple maze to test a turtle's intelligence. The maze had seven possible turns, four of them wrong. To reach food and water the turtle had to find its way through. After a while it learned to make its way without a single error—but this took thirty-eight tries.

Study of turtles' anatomy has shown that actually they have well-developed ears. Strangely, however, they don't seem to use them. Experiments seem to prove that turtles just don't hear air-borne sounds. Instead, they rely on vibrations carried through the earth or water. Speak to a turtle and it will pay no heed; hit the ground or water nearby and it will notice.

Turtles have fairly good eyesight, and a very good sense of smell. In fact, if some scientists are right, the turtle's sense of smell is truly wonderful. We'll look at this more carefully in another chapter.

2. Sea Turtles

Turtles that spend most of their lives in the open sea are divided by scientists into two families. The giant leatherback, the biggest of all living turtles, is put in a family of its own called Dermochelidae. The other family, called Cheloniidae, includes four major groups, or genera, of turtles, each with its own scientific name. These are: the loggerheads, *Caretta*; the green turtles, *Chelonia*; the ridleys, *Lepidochelys*; and the hawksbill turtles, *Eretmochelys*. Each of these genera, in turn, contains one or more individual species, and each species has a second scientific name to identify it. For instances, *Caretta caretta* is the common loggerhead; *Lepidochelys kempi* is the ridley commonly called the Atlantic ridley. Closely related species and subspecies will have a third and even a fourth name, but we are not going to bother with those in this book.

Whatever the name, some species of sea turtles are found in all the warm waters of the world. In fact, some have been found in fairly cold water—off Nova Scotia and in the far South Atlantic—but they may have gotten there by mistake rather than intent.

NATURE'S MOST AMAZING INVENTION

Living in the ocean, these turtles have needed to make certain changes from their land-dwelling relatives. The sea turtle's shell tends to be somewhat lighter and not quite so rigid. But the main difference is in the legs. The sea turtle's legs have changed

19

All sea turtle eggs look much like Ping-Pong balls. However, the egg of the leatherback, Dermochelys coriacea, *will sometimes have one or more green spots. Just why, nobody knows.*

into flippers. With these it can outswim many fish. On land, the sea turtle moves very slowly and with great effort. Breathing is difficult. Despite its great size—and all of them are large—the sea turtle on land is almost helpless. Turned on its back—"turned turtle," as the old saying goes—it cannot right itself and is completely helpless.

Even so, the sea turtle—at least, the female sea turtle—must come ashore at times. The reason for this takes some explaining.

Countless millions of years ago the ancestors of today's turtles, like those of all animals, lived in the sea. Little by little some animals learned to take oxygen from the air rather than from water. Gradually they came to live most of their lives on land. But the females had to go back into the water to lay their eggs. Left on land, the eggs would have quickly dried, the tiny speck of life within each would have died. Then somehow—no man can say how—reptiles developed an egg that could be left on land. Some scientists now call this "nature's most amazing invention." Without it, animal life would have been forever tied to the sea.

The outside of this amazing invention is the shell. It is tough and hard enough to protect the matter inside, yet porous enough to allow the passage of oxygen. Inside is the single cell, fertilized by the male sperm, that will become an animal. Around this speck of life is a sac called the *amnion*. This is filled with a fluid that protects the life inside, giving it a pond of its own in which to develop. Scientists call this the amniotic egg. Turtles were among the first animals to develop it.

Later, many millions of years later, some turtles would go back to live in the sea. Again, no one knows just why. But the females still must come ashore to lay their eggs.

This applies to all sea turtles. And it is a dangerous and difficult time.

The green turtle

The green turtle, *Chelonia mydas*, isn't really green. Actually its shell is dark brown or almost black. (It's the faintly greenish color of the fat that gives this turtle its name.)

Of all the sea turtles, the green turtle is the most prized as food by human beings. Because green turtle soup and steaks are so good, *Chelonia mydas* has been fiercely hunted and killed. For the same reason it has been carefully studied by herpetologists who want to protect it, both for itself and as an important source of food for many people. Many of the things learned about the green turtle are also true of other sea turtles.

Nesting

It is nearly always night when the green turtle comes ashore to lay her eggs. In the pounding surf it is almost impossible to see her, even under a full moon. Then, as the waves pull back, leaving her on the wet sand, the big, dark form becomes visible. On the average she will weigh about three hundred pounds, with a shell three feet long.

At the edge of the surf the turtle stops. Carefully she studies the beach, her head turning from one side to the other. It may be that she is smelling the air, the beach itself, as well as looking. A sudden light, a movement, will send her back into the sea. But if all seems well, she lowers her head and begins her clumsy struggle across the sand.

Her nesting place must be beyond the high-tide mark. The shells of the eggs are porous; if they become water-soaked, the unborn turtles will drown. However, the nest must not be too far from the water. When the eggs hatch, the farther the baby turtles must crawl to reach the water, the greater their danger. Usually the female will pick a spot near the vegetation line. Here she makes a wide sweep with one of her front flippers, testing the sand.

With the spot chosen, the female begins to dig. Before this, a light a hundred feet away would have sent her back into the sea. Now she becomes totally unconscious of everything but

This is the green turtle, Chelonia mydas, *in the process of laying her eggs at night on a beach in Surinam, South America. Notice the carefully shaped hole in which the eggs are placed.*

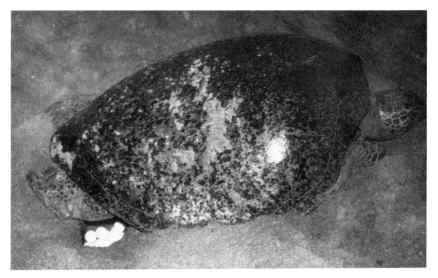

digging. A watcher may shine a flashlight directly into her eyes. A child may sit on her back. She will not notice. Using her front flippers, she sends the sand flying.

The depth of this body pit—finished, it is just big enough to hold the body of the female turtle—is extremely important. It determines the final depth at which the eggs will be laid. This depth must be enough to protect the eggs. It must keep them at the right temperature with the right amount of moisture. These things the turtle knows by instinct. Sometimes she may make an error, but not often.

With the body pit finished, the turtle begins to use her hind flippers. Curling them into scoops, she very carefully dips out the sand. The hole she digs now is bottle-shaped, with the large part at the bottom. This is the actual nest in which the eggs will be placed. It is just as deep as the turtle can reach with her hind flippers.

When the nest is complete, the female begins to lay her eggs. These are about the size of Ping-Pong balls and look much like them. The shells are leathery rather than being hard and brittle like those of a hen. While laying, the female is as unconscious of what goes on around her as she had been while digging the nest. Raccoons, wild dogs, even people have taken a turtle's eggs while she laid them, the turtle never looking.

The green turtle will lay, on the average, about one hundred eggs at a time. When the job is finished, she carefully covers the nest. With great sweeps of her flippers she spreads the sand to hide the place. Satisfied at last, she heads once more for the water's edge. She moves slowly, tired from her work. Her breathing is heavy. But when she enters the water things are different. She moves both front flippers at the same time, like a person swimming the breast stroke. Now she is at home. A green turtle can easily swim as fast as a man can walk. For short distances they have been timed at twenty miles an hour. Swiftly

This is the track the female green turtle, Chelonia mydas, *leaves on returning to the sea after nesting. The exact position of the nest has, however, been carefully hidden. This one had nested on a beach in Mexico.*

the female heads toward the open sea.

A short distance offshore a great school of males are waiting to mate with her and with other females returning from the beach.

THE MATING OF GREEN TURTLES

Once a male green turtle of the Caribbean or Atlantic Ocean has hatched and gone to sea, it never comes ashore again. So the mating of all green turtles—indeed, of all sea turtles—takes place in the water.

This occurs near the nesting beaches. But it may be either before or after the female goes ashore to lay her eggs. And, strangely, her next clutch of eggs may not have been fertilized at this time. Scientists believe the female turtle may carry the live sperm from one mating for two or even three years before laying the eggs.

In mating, the male climbs onto the back of the female, holding himself there with two long claws, one on each front flipper.

This is a male green turtle. Normally these males never come ashore after they have hatched and gone to sea. However, mating takes place just off the nesting beach. This one was captured by herpetologists and dragged into shallow water to be tagged and then released.

Possibly the male may also use his jaws; at least, females coming ashore to lay eggs often have deep scars in their shells. But since both turtles must breathe air, there is a great rolling and tumbling. Much of this is underwater. As a result, herpetologists have never been able to study accurately the mating of sea turtles.

The female green turtle will lay more than one clutch of eggs in a season. In fact, she may come ashore to lay every two weeks or so during a summer. In this way the female may lay five hundred eggs or even more in one summer. However, she does not return to the nesting beach the next summer. Some females nest every other summer, some every third summer. But none comes back every year.

With the end of the season, both the males and females disappear from the waters near the nesting beach. Their eggs are left behind, forgotten, buried in the sand.

THE BABY TURTLES

Once a turtle egg has been laid and warmed by the sun, the speck of life inside grows amazingly fast. Within one day the single fertilized cell will become a million cells, or more. Within a few days there is a tiny heart beating and blood flowing through veins. Little by little the baby turtle takes shape. Its ribs and backbone move to the outside of its small, soft body. They grow together and begin to harden. Within about sixty days, depending on the warmth soaking down through the sand, the baby turtle is fully formed, about two inches long, and ready to break out of its shell.

On the nose of each unborn turtle there is a sharp bump called an egg tooth. Later this will disappear, but now the baby, wiggling and twisting, uses this egg tooth to break out of the egg. And since all the eggs were laid at practically the same time, most of them will hatch at the same time. But how do they,

Baby green turtles, Chelonia mydas, *newly hatched, head for the open sea.*

newly born, find their way from beneath the hard-packed sand to the open air?

Dr. Archie Carr of the University of Florida has spent many years studying turtles, particularly green turtles. To learn how the babies hatched, Dr. Carr carefully dug the sand from one side of a turtle's nest. He replaced it with a pane of clear glass. And then he waited.

The first turtles to cut free of their eggs lay still and rested. Then as more and more were born, the job of digging themselves out began. For each baby turtle it was, probably, no more than wiggling and squirming, much like the action that had broken it free of the egg. But all together it was a kind of blind, instinctive teamwork.

The turtles at the top of the pile shook down the sand from

the top. Those around the sides also brought down loose sand. The wiggling turtles at the bottom packed the sand down—and in doing this they raised themselves and the others toward the top.

Now and then a turtle would stop work. Sometimes all of them might pause. Then one near the bottom would begin to squirm and kick. Like a signal, this set off the others. The sand kept drifting down from top and sides. The turtles at the bottom kept packing it down—until all at once the surface seemed to explode baby turtles. "Like corn out of a popper," Dr. Carr said.

To test the importance of this instinctive teamwork, Dr. Carr buried a number of turtle eggs alongside glass plates where he could watch. When only one or two were placed together, the baby turtles usually died without reaching the surface. But where ten or more were put together, nearly all of them broke free safely.

When the baby turtles crawl out onto the beach they start instinctively for the ocean. They may be behind sand dunes or driftwood where the water is invisible. Yet, almost without fail, they go in the right direction. And here too the number of turtles born together is important. A single baby on the beach may seem uncertain. Or he may tend to loaf—a very dangerous thing in a baby turtle's life, as we'll see. But where there are many babies, the loafers get pushed along; the uncertain ones join the group. And the whole mass moves as rapidly as possible toward the water.

Just how a newborn turtle knows which way to go is uncertain. Herpetologists now believe that light has something to do with it. If taken a hundred yards or more inland, the babies will, normally, still head for the sea. But if they are put down where trees block the view of the sky above the ocean, they seem confused. If there is a lake and open sky in another direction, they may go that way. Also baby turtles born at night

Probably the most dangerous time in a turtle's life is from the moment it breaks out of the egg until it makes its wobbling way across the beach to the water. And its most dangerous enemy may be the sea gull. In vast numbers, they dive screaming on the baby turtles.

near a highway sometimes crawl toward the lights of passing cars.

But usually a baby, breaking free of the nest made by its mother, heads for the water. And if there is ever a time when a turtle needs to hurry, this is it.

In some places wild dogs, pigs, even buzzards and sea gulls seem to know ahead of time when the eggs will hatch. They gather in great numbers. And as the baby turtles creep across the wet sand toward the water, their enemies descend on them.

Jacques Cousteau, a French naturalist, once saw an estimated 250,000 turtles hatch within a few days on the beach of an uninhabited island. Sea gulls attacked them in countless numbers. There were so many gulls they almost blotted out the sky.

Screaming, whirling round and round, they dived on the baby turtles. Cousteau and his men tried to drive the gulls away, but it was hopeless. When it was all over, Cousteau estimated that not more than 1,000 of all the baby turtles had escaped.

Turtles that hatch at night have a better chance than those hatched during the day. But even those that reach the sea are not safe. The small turtle is an excellent dish for schools of mackerel, bonito, and many other fish. No one knows what percentage of the babies live even to start growing up. But surely it is a small number.

Once in the water, the baby turtle heads straight out to sea. It swims strongly, using its foreflippers in a kind of breast stroke, exactly like its parents.

And then it disappears.

This is true not only of the baby green turtle; it is true of most sea turtles. And it is one of the great unsolved scientific mysteries: where do sea turtles go during the first year or so of their lives?

Fishermen hauling nets near the nesting beaches sometimes catch baby turtles. But this is only during the hatching season. At no other time of the year are they found in the area. But neither are they found anywhere else.

It may be that there simply are not many baby sea turtles compared to the larger ones. Born in great numbers, they are also destroyed in great numbers. Also, those that live grow rapidly. Probably within two years they are large enough to be safe from most of their enemies. After this they will keep living, and growing, for a long time.

So maybe there are not a great many sea turtles more than two or three days old, and less than a year or so. However, there must be some. Where do they live?

Off the west coast of Florida near Cedar Key there are large expanses of shallow water. The bottom here is thickly grown with marine grasses. And here, every summer, a number of young green turtles can be found feeding. But the average size of these turtles is about thirty pounds. They are probably three or four years old. Certainly none of them are very young. Nor are they fully grown. None of the females contain eggs. If turtles travel in schools, this might be called an elementary school.

They appear in the spring and disappear in the fall. Where they come from and where they go, no one can say.

Much more is known about the migrations of adult sea turtles. Yet there is a mystery here also, even more puzzling than the disappearance of the young.

All sea turtles like to nest on beaches that are pounded by surf and washed by strong tides. Such action tends to pile up the deep sand needed for nests. However, it also tends to scrub the offshore bottom clean of vegetation. And the adult green turtle needs such underwater grasses for food. So the feeding grounds of the green turtle must be away from the nesting grounds. Indeed, they may be a thousand miles or more.

How then does the female turtle, swimming in the open sea, pushed this way and that by currents and tides, find her way back to the exact same beach, and sometimes to almost the same spot on that beach, every two or three years to lay her eggs? To add to the mystery, this is probably the same beach where this female broke out of an egg years before.

No one can say with certainty that females return to the same beaches where they were hatched. This is because no one has yet found a way to put a mark on a baby turtle that will still be recognizable when that turtle is mature, seven or eight years later and some three hundred pounds heavier. Naturalists have tried tagging and tattooing; even magnets have been inserted into the baby turtles. But the tags and tattoos disappear, and the magnets had to be so small that later it was impossible to detect them.

However, it is fairly easy to tag the mature female turtle when she comes ashore to lay her eggs. And in this way it has been learned that the same female will come ashore on the same beach every second or third year.

Many green turtles have been tagged while nesting on Ascension Island in the South Atlantic. These same turtles will be found later, grazing on pastures of turtle grass off the coast of northern Brazil, 1,400 miles away. Each December many of them disappear from their Brazilian pastures. And about eight weeks later they start to crawl ashore on the beaches of Ascension.

Ascension Island has only thirty-four square miles of area. It is a mere speck in the vast reaches of the South Atlantic. How can the turtles possibly find their way?

Part of the answer may lie in what is called the Sea Floor Spreading Theory. According to this, Africa and South America were once joined together. Then, about a hundred million years ago, they began to break apart. The ancient North Atlantic Ocean pushed between them, grew wider and wider.

Turtles, which have been around for some two hundred million years or more, may have nested on some island in the slowly widening gap. At that time it would have been only a short trip from such an island to the pastures of turtle grass almost due westward. Generation after generation made the journey, directed by the rising or setting sun. But gradually the journey grew longer. Also, one island might eventually disappear beneath the sea while volcanoes would create another. This new island might be in the same general direction, but not exactly. So something more exact than a course set by the sun must help the turtles to their final landing.

Turtles heading east from Brazil would, somewhere along the way, cross a major ocean current that flows past Ascension. Some naturalists believe that this current carries with it a quality that makes it different from other currents. It may be an odor. And built into the turtle is an ability to recognize this quality, to remember it from when, newly hatched, this turtle first entered the ocean. Then the turtle would turn and follow the current back to its birthplace.

The largest nesting ground for green turtles in the Americas is at Tortuguero Beach on the east coast of Costa Rica. Scientists have been studying these turtles for a number of years. The females they tagged at Tortuguero have later been found all over the Caribbean Sea. In returning to their home beach these turtles cannot all follow a single compass course. Yet they do return. And as the females drag themselves out of the surf, they stop. They turn their heads as if smelling not only the air but the beach itself.

So a sense of smell may have some part in the sea turtle's ability to navigate a thousand miles of open sea and return to its birthplace. But that ability remains one of nature's great unsolved mysteries.

THE LOGGERHEAD

If turtles were people, you might call the loggerhead, *Caretta caretta*, a "character." It has a distinct look and personality all its own. Its shell is more red, or reddish brown, in color than that of other turtles, and its big head is unusually round.

Except for the giant leatherback, the loggerhead may be the biggest of all living turtles. It sometimes grows to weigh a thousand pounds or more, with a shell four feet across, and a skull almost a foot wide. But the average nesting female is much smaller, usually about two hundred to three hundred pounds.

The temper and actions of a loggerhead are unpredictable. A school of them swimming free in the ocean seem to play like children: they roll and splash and crawl over one another. One naturalist referred to their "elfin drollery," and another to their

This is the mating of two loggerhead turtles, Caretta caretta, *photographed at Marineland, Florida. The long claw on the front flipper by which the male holds himself in position is not visible in this picture.*

"good humor." Divers have swum among them for hours without harm.

But not always.

Not long ago two scuba divers off Key West were suddenly "attacked" by a number of loggerheads. For a time it looked as if they might be drowned by turtles swimming into and over them. One man was severely bitten before he could get back to his boat.

Reporters who heard the story consulted Dr. Archie Carr and were surprised when he began to laugh. "I don't think these turtles were trying to injure the divers," he said. "I think they were trying to mate with them." Loggerheads, he said, often nest in the Florida Keys. And like the green turtles, loggerheads mate in the waters near the nesting beaches. "Probably the divers met a number of male turtles," Dr. Carr said. "And it's possible these mistook the divers for female loggerheads. What might be a little love nip between turtles could be a serious wound for a person."

If the male loggerheads had been angry rather than amorous, the divers might have fared much worse than they did, for the huge loggerhead can be a dangerous enemy. The New York *Herald* of September 3, 1905, told of a battle between a loggerhead and a boatload of men:

Five East Norwalk fishermen crawled into port last evening, using the stumps of their oars as paddles, and with one of their number unconscious on the bottom of the boat as a result of an attempt to catch the famous 610 pound loggerhead turtle which had escaped from Captain Charles E. Ducross, a South Norwalk marketman, and which was the largest and most vicious turtle of this species ever brought into Fulton Market. . . .

Charles Ducross offered a $50 reward for the recapture of the turtle, and Frank Petty and his sons, Frank and George, and two other men named Swanson set out yesterday in a rowboat intending to catch the chelonian . . .

The Petty party found the turtle asleep in the harbor . . . They approached him slowly and cautiously. Swanson, who is an expert fisherman and sailor, attempted to drive an eel spear, to which a long and heavy line was attached, through the back of the turtle. The spear broke off short in the tough shell of the turtle and then there commenced a fight which lasted nearly an hour.

The chelonian seemed to have no fear of the men or the boat. He turned upon them and with his flippers almost overturned the boat. The five men beat him over the head with the oars. These he occasionally got in his mouth and each in turn was crushed and broken off. It was in the thickest of the fight that Swanson was struck either by one of the flippers of the animal or by his beak, and a long gash was torn in his arm. In spite of his wound Swanson assisted in the fight until the turtle withdrew and sank from sight, apparently none the worse for his encounter.

It took the party nearly two hours to paddle their craft, which was nearly full of water, back to port. They say they do not intend to try to capture any more loggerheads, reward or no reward. . .

The loggerheads are as unpredictable in their travels as in their disposition. They have been found off Canada and off the coast of Ireland. One was found far up the Mississippi River. It might have been lost, but this is doubtful. Loggerheads, like other sea turtles, can navigate thousands of miles of open ocean to find one small nesting beach.

In their far wanderings the loggerheads seem able to feed on whatever is available. Basically they are meat-eaters, crunching shrimp, crabs, and small fish in their powerful jaws. But like the green turtle, they sometimes eat marine grasses, or even seaweed. In the open sea loggerheads have been seen to swim through a mass of Portuguese men-of-war, calmly munching on the barbed and poisonous tentacles as they went.

The meat of the loggerhead is not as tasty as that of the green turtle, and so it has been less hunted by human beings. But wild animals dig up and eat the eggs in vast numbers. On Cape Sable in the Everglades National Park raccoons in one year destroyed 140 out of 199 nests that naturalists had located.

Fortunately for the loggerhead, most of those that live in the Atlantic nest on beaches along the east coast of Florida. One of the most popular of these is on Jupiter Island. Here an organization called the Turtle Boys of Jupiter Island patrols the beach during the nesting season. Some of the nests are guarded against animal predators, or the eggs may be dug up and reburied where they can be protected. When the babies hatch, they are raised in artificial ponds until big enough to have a better chance of survival. Each year the Turtle Boys raise an average of thirty thousand loggerheads in these ponds.

THE RIDLEYS

All sea turtles have their unsolved mysteries, but the ridleys have more than their share.

For a long time naturalists argued among themselves as to whether or not there really was such a thing as a ridley. Some people thought it might be a different species of loggerhead. Some thought the loggerhead sometimes crossbred with a green or maybe a hawksbill turtle: the ridley, they said, was a result of crossbreeding. Eventually, however, it was determined that the ridley was truly a genus of its own. In fact, there were two species of ridleys, *Lepidochelys kempi* in the Atlantic and *Lepidochelys olivacea* in the Pacific.

The ridley is the smallest of the sea turtles, rarely weighing over 150 or 160 pounds. The carapace is slightly rounder than that of the loggerhead, which tapers toward the rear. The Atlantic ridley is gray; the Pacific ridley an olive green, and is often commonly called the olive ridley. There are several differences in the bones, but it requires an autopsy to see this.

Once the herpetologists knew the ridley was a genus of its own, there was a new and even greater mystery. The Pacific ridley was known to nest in a number of different places. But where did the Atlantic ridley nest?

Along the coast of Florida and the Carolinas, fishermen sometimes caught ridleys in their nets. Now and then ridleys showed up as far north as Massachusetts. But no naturalist knew where or if they went ashore to nest.

Actually there were people who knew the nesting place of

37

the ridley, but they were not scientists. They did not know the turtle was a ridley. They knew the thing that took place was a great wonder, but they did not know it was a scientific mystery.

One of these was a well-to-do Mexican named Señor Andrés Herrera. Señor Herrera had a great interest in nature, but no scientific training. When he heard a Mexican peasant tell about a place where turtles nested, in the daytime, by many thousands, he was interested but doubtful. He began to ask other peasants from the same part of the country.

Between Tampico, Mexico, and the Texas border there is a stretch of beach some ninety miles long. Almost uninhabited at this time, there were miles and miles without a house of any kind. It was here, Señor Herrera was told, that the turtles nested. They did not always come ashore at exactly the same place. Nor did they come ashore at exactly the same time each year. It was, however, somewhere along this beach between the first of April and the end of June.

Señor Herrera wanted to see this wonderful thing. He had a small airplane and each day he flew up the beach and back again. For twenty-four days he saw nothing. On the twenty-fifth day, skimming low over the beach, he saw a thing he could not believe. Ahead of him the entire beach was moving, crawling, a solid mass of life.

Herrera stared. As far as he could see there were turtles. Nothing but turtles. A man could have walked on their backs for a solid mile without touching the sand. Herrera turned back to where the beach was clear, and landed. He got out of his plane with a camera.

Turtles were coming out of the sea in such numbers they crawled over one another. They butted head-on into turtles crawling back into the Gulf of Mexico. Those turtles beyond the high-tide mark were digging nests. They threw up such a storm of sand it was difficult to see through.

38

There were three or four Mexican peasants on the beach gathering eggs. They were men who lived in the general area. They called this great gathering of turtles *arribada*, meaning "the arrival."

Señor Herrera took motion pictures of the spectacle. Then he flew home. There he showed the pictures to some of his friends, none of whom were herpetologists. After awhile he forgot them.

Almost twenty years later, in 1961, a Dr. Henry Hildebrand of the University of Corpus Christi was studying sea life along the Gulf Coast of Mexico. He heard of Señor Herrera and his motion pictures. Hildebrand visited Herrera and saw the pictures. He could scarcely believe what he saw. So he borrowed the film to exhibit at a meeting of zoologists. They identified the turtles: there could be no doubt that they were ridleys—forty thousand or more of them at one time!

So the mystery of a nesting place for the Atlantic ridley was solved. But this opened the door to other unknowns. Why did these turtles nest in the daytime rather than at night like all other sea turtles? And where did they come from in such vast numbers? No one had ever seen any huge school of these turtles swimming together. To this day, no one ever has. Yet forty thousand or more arrived at one spot at one time.

Six years after Henry Hildebrand saw Señor Herrera's motion pictures, Dr. Peter Pritchard was tagging turtles on the coast of Surinam in South America. Green turtles, loggerheads, even some giant leatherbacks nested on the beach where he worked, but no ridleys. Then from the Indians helping him, Dr. Pritchard began to hear stories of a slightly different kind of turtle. It nested on a beach to the south of where he worked. And it came ashore in large numbers.

Dr. Pritchard went to see, and arrived just in time. The turtles were crawling out of the sea, and they were ridleys. An *arribada*. But there was a difference from the one along the coast of

The nesting turtle is the olive or Pacific ridley, photographed in South America.

Mexico. These ridleys started ashore in the late afternoon, and continued during the night. They came by the hundreds rather than the thousands—a very small *arribada* compared to the other.

Dr. Pritchard was in for a still greater surprise. These ridleys were nesting on a beach of the Atlantic Ocean—but they were not Atlantic ridleys. They were *Lepidochelys olivacea*, the olive or Pacific ridley. The difference between the two species is slight, but distinct. The Atlantic ridley has five big scales on each side of the carapace; the Pacific ridley has six or more.

Still later it would be learned that the Pacific ridley also nested on the Atlantic coast of Africa, but did not nest on the Pacific coast of Africa. It nested in many other places around the Pacific and Indian oceans, including the Pacific coast of Mexico.

In all these places the ridleys nested separately or in comparatively small numbers. Large schools of ridleys had been seen swimming off the coasts of California and Mexico, but there were no known *arribadas*. Where these turtles went no one knew. Then, very recently, scientists found a desolate beach on the Pacific coast of Costa Rica. The beach itself was rather small, only about 180,000 square feet. Here, during a great *arribada* that lasted, off and on, for over two months, an estimated 290,000 nests were dug and 29 million eggs were laid. The last turtles to arrive simply dug up and destroyed the eggs of earlier ridleys in order to lay their own.

THE HAWKSBILL

The hawksbill, *Eretmochelys imbricata*, is well named. It has powerful jaws with a narrow head and a beak shaped much like that of a hawk. Next to the ridley, this is the smallest of the sea turtles. On an average, a fully grown hawksbill won't go much over a hundred pounds.

In the struggle for survival the hawksbill has even more problems than most turtles. It is the only one that can be turned into what is called tortoiseshell jewelry.

The laminae—the scales—of the hawksbill are thicker than those of any other turtle. On the living hawksbill these have no

This is a young hawksbill, Eretmochelys imbricata. *Sea turtles of this age are rare. They turn up only now and then. Where most young sea turtles spend their time is unknown. Notice hawk bill shape of the beak.*

particular shine. But off the turtle they take a high polish, gleaming with yellow, gold, olive, and black. Heated, two or more can be molded together to give added thickness, and they can be bent and carved into various shapes.

Long before the time of Christ, tortoiseshell jewelry was popular in India, China, and Japan. Gradually its use spread westward. The Roman Emperor Nero had an entire bathtub made of tortoiseshell—which may be the biggest one piece of tortoiseshell in history.

Normally the hawksbill is killed before the scales are removed. Then boiling water or very hot ash is poured over the carapace, and the hot scales peeled off. Some primitive people, however, poured their boiling water, or even built fires, on the backs of the living turtles. This was in the belief that scales from a living turtle were more beautiful than those from a turtle that had been killed. Also, it was believed that the turtle when returned to the sea would grow a new shell.

In fact, the boiling water or even a small fire did not immediately kill the turtle. But once in the sea without its tough shell for protection, it might easily be killed by sharks or other large fish. Even if not attacked, it would probably become diseased and die.

Hunted for its shell as well as its food, the hawksbill might well have been wiped out except for two things. Now and then the meat of the hawksbill is poisonous. And there's no way for the would-be turtle-eater to know this except by trying. The hawksbill itself feeds along the bottom of shallow waters and around coral reefs. Apparently it eats almost anything it comes on—shellfish, seaweed, mangrove roots, sponges, jellyfish. Some of the sponges and other plantlike animals found along the reefs are poisonous. And this is probably the reason the meat of the hawksbill is sometimes, though not often, also poisonous.

Far more important in the survival of the hawksbill is its

method of nesting. Of all the sea turtles it is the least likely to nest in large numbers close together. Sometimes a few may come ashore on one beach at one time. But usually their nests are scattered over tropic beaches around the world. This makes it difficult for the turtle hunters to destroy them in large numbers.

Still, as the price of tortoiseshell jewelry goes higher and higher, the hawksbill is hunted more and more. Whether or not it will continue to survive no one can say at this time.

THE LEATHERBACK

Like the hawksbill, the leatherback turtle, *Dermochelys coriacea*, is well named. Of all the sea turtles the leatherback is the only one without a hard, rocklike shell. Instead, both the carapace and plastron look and feel like leather. Imbedded in this is a mass of small, flat bones, and these, along with the leathery covering, make up a kind of shell that is sometimes two inches thick.

Leatherbacks are the biggest of all turtles—land or sea. They often weigh 1,000 to 1,300 pounds. Some have been said to weigh 2,000 pounds, but it's doubtful if anybody ever actually weighed one of that size. They have been measured, however, at eleven feet from the tip of one front flipper to the tip of the other, with a carapace nine feet long.

Despite its huge size, the jaws of the leatherback are extremely weak. The barnacles and shellfish that other sea turtles happily nibble on would break the jaws of a leatherback. Instead, it seems to live almost entirely on jellyfish. Since jellyfish are almost all water, it takes a lot of them for a 1,300-pound turtle. Searching for them, the leatherback spends most of its life traveling the high seas rather than feeding along reefs or pastures of marine grasses.

The leatherback's skull, like the frame of its shell, is not one large bone but many small ones. In fact, the skull of a dead

43

leatherback will eventually fall into a jumble of small pieces with no obvious shape.

Until 1968 herpetologists believed that most of the world's leatherbacks nested on a single beach in Malaysia. Then Dr. Peter Pritchard discovered a new nesting ground in French Guiana on the Atlantic coast of South America. The leatherbacks here did not quite make an *arribada* like the ridleys of Mexico. But every night all summer long one hundred, sometimes two and three hundred, giants would labor out of the surf to lay their eggs. Some of the females came ashore to lay as many as eight times in one season, an average of eighty-six eggs each time. By the end of the season the beach was so filled with eggs that almost every fifth turtle dug up an old nest to make a new one.

Like all sea turtles except the ridley on the coast of Mexico, the leatherbacks nest at night. This is probably because sea

A leatherback, Dermochelys coriacea, *the biggest of all living turtles. This one in Surinam, South America, has laid her eggs, been tagged by herpetologists studying its nesting habits, and is now returning to the sea.*

A baby leatherback turtle, Dermochelys coriacea, *breaking out of its shell. Normally this would happen while the egg is still buried in the sand. This one was removed as it began to hatch in order to photograph.*

turtles dry out quickly. On dry land under a tropic sun the sea turtle will soon die. (How the Atlantic ridley manages is just another of its mysteries.)

The leatherback seems to have one advantage over other sea turtles. Her own body odor appears to hide the odor of her eggs. Wild pigs and other would-be egg-eaters rarely find the nest of a leatherback.

On the other hand, because of her soft shell, the female is sometimes killed by jaguars on the beach. But for a jaguar this is not easy. A thousand-pound leatherback can give a powerful blow with her flippers.

Dr. Pritchard and his assistants quickly learned this when they set out to tag the leatherbacks. Panting slowly back toward the sea, the females sometimes stop to rest. This, or while in the act of laying, was the time to apply the tag. Otherwise the leatherback might simply keep crawling, taking the tagging pliers with her. Or she might use a flipper to knock the tagger heels over head.

Herpetologists estimate there are only thirty thousand to forty thousand female leatherbacks in all the world. (Since the males never come ashore there is no way to estimate their number.) A few nest individually on tropic beaches around the world. But probably half of all the leatherbacks nest on the beach in French Guiana.

Part of this beach is littered with the stumps of dead mangrove

A young leatherback, Dermochelys coriacea, *raised at the Miami Sea-quarium. Leatherbacks of this age are very rare, and only recently has there been any success in raising them in captivity.*

trees. As the female leatherback comes panting ashore she is often blocked by these trees. Because of her huge size, and moving on flippers meant for swimming, not walking, she cannot back up. However, she can turn slowly to right or left. Nearly always she finds her way past the dead trees to the part of the beach where she wants to nest.

When her eggs are laid, the female does not follow her own tracks back to the water. Instead, she heads directly for the ocean. Once again she may find her way blocked. Sometimes she keeps pushing head-on into the stump or log until she has no room left to turn. She cannot back up. And so she is trapped. Unless the tide comes in and lifts her, she may stay here and die, so close to the open sea that the spray blows across her.

Baby leatherbacks hatching on this same beach have a curious method of finding their way. Each one, as soon as it reaches the surface, crawls in a small but complete circle. No other sea turtle does this. Then, having once observed the full circle of the sky, the baby knows which direction to go. Like the mother, it must make its way past logs and stumps. But being only two or three inches long instead of seven feet or more, it does not need as much room to turn. Unless a gull or some other animal catches it first, the baby will probably make it to the ocean.

And there it simply disappears until it is almost grown. Even less is known about the immature leatherback, along with the olive or Pacific ridley, than about the young of other sea turtles.

3. Diamondback Terrapins

The diamondback terrapin, *Malaclemys terrapin*, is not a far-roaming, deep-sea turtle like the leatherback, the green, and other big saltwater relatives. But neither is it a true freshwater turtle. Instead, it lives in the brackish water of salt marshes, and along the edges of bays and inlets where salt and fresh water mix. If captured and kept in nothing but fresh water it is likely to develop a fungus and die. In its natural home it can swim like a fish, but always stays close to land.

In at least one way the diamondback is the most famous of turtles. This was the turtle (it's usually called a terrapin) from which the delicious and most highly priced terrapin stew was made. Never more than eight or nine inches long, these turtles once sold for as much as ninety dollars a dozen. And this was around the turn of the century when a dollar bought a lot more than it does now.

Because of the price, the hunting of diamondbacks became important business. Where the winters are cold, the diamondbacks dig into the mud of a salt marsh and hibernate. But some people claim that the very best stew was made from turtles dug out of the mud. As a result they were hunted all year long. Originally found along the coast from Massachusetts to Florida and west to Texas, they were soon in danger of being wiped out.

Terrapin stew is truly delicious, but for most persons it never was really worth the price. Some people ate it merely to show off, and gradually it lost popularity. It is still served in many

This is the diamondback terrapin from which terrapin stew is made. Never growing to more than eight or nine inches, they once sold for up to ninety dollars a dozen.

places, still good, and still expensive. But now most of these diamondback terrapins are raised on "turtle farms" in the Maryland area rather than caught wild.

The diamondback is easy to recognize. The laminae on its back are clearly grooved in lopsided diamond shapes. The pale skin of its neck and legs is sprinkled with spots. Its legs are neither the paddle-like affairs of the sea turtles, nor the tree-trunk legs of the pure land turtles. Instead, its legs are somewhere between. The clawed toes are webbed for swimming, but the stubby legs are more like those of the land turtles. This is true of freshwater turtles in general.

49

4. The Soft-Shell Turtles

The giant leatherback turtle might be called a soft-shell—certainly its shell is softer than that of the other sea turtles. Technically, however, the name "soft-shell" belongs to another group of turtles. There are about twenty-seven species, scattered over most of the tropic and temperate world. All of them spend most of their lives in fresh water, some in ponds or swamps, some in running streams. All look very much alike. They tend to be round and flat; many people call them pancake turtles. They have long, snorkel-like snouts, soft shells, and mean tempers.

The shell of the soft-shell is more like leather than bone. Around the edges it is soft enough to bend easily downward. This helps the animal bury itself quickly in sand or mud, leaving only its eyes and its nostrils exposed. Here it is almost impossible to see, either by some animal that might want to feed on the turtle, or by the small fish, frogs, and insects that the turtle feeds on.

Because its soft shell does not give this turtle as much protection as a bony carapace, the soft-shell turtle has another means of defense. These turtles have soft, fleshy looking lips—but don't let that fool you into putting your fingers close to them. Back of those lips is a beak like a razor blade and jaws like a vise. With its long neck, the soft-shell can strike as swiftly as a snake.

People in the South used to say that if a soft-shell turtle bit you, it would not let go until it thundered. That may be an exaggeration, but it does tend to hold on. And its beak can make

The soft-shell turtle's nose is at the end of its snout, with eyes close by, so it can breathe and look around while the rest of its body is hidden. Notice the webbed feet for swimming.

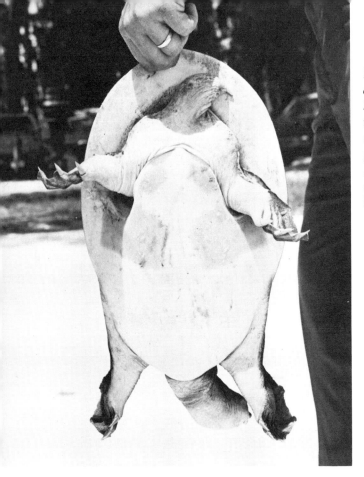

If you are going to pick up a soft-shell, this—or using both hands together—is the way to do it. But be sure to hold it well away from your body. The soft-shell has almost no tail, but a long neck and can strike like a snake.

a nasty cut on a hand or finger.

Some of the biting turtles have long tails by which they can be handled safely—as long as you hold them well away from your body. The soft-shell has almost no tail. If you are going to pick one up, use both hands and grip it at the back of the carapace, between the hind legs. On the other hand, it is probably best to leave a soft-shell turtle alone, unless you know exactly what you're doing.

In the United States soft-shells can be found in ponds and streams almost anywhere east of the Rocky Mountains. There are four species, but except to the trained herpetologist there isn't much difference among them. The southern soft-shell,

Trionyx ferox—some scientists call it *Amyda ferox*—may grow to be eighteen inches long and weigh thirty pounds or more. The northern soft-shell, *Trionyx spiniferus* or *Amyda spiniferus,* never gets quite that big. Also the northern species has tiny bumps on its shell, making it feel like sandpaper. It is these little spines that give it the second part of its scientific name. Actually they are what is left of the scales that all reptiles are supposed to have.

Both species are basically meat-eaters, feeding on small fish, crawfish, even small birds. People who raise ducks don't want soft-shell turtles in their ponds.

Like all other turtles, the soft-shell must come to land to lay her eggs. Nearly always she chooses a spot close to the water. Here the southern soft-shell buries herself right up to her nose. And here she stays until the laying is complete—an act that some people say takes several days.

One of the largest soft-shells, *Chitra indica*, lives in India. This species often gets to be three feet in length. Some people say they grow to be six feet long. In fact, there are stories about this turtle attacking and sinking small boats.

In other parts of India various species of soft-shells are thought to be sacred. They are kept in ponds and fed by their worshipers. In some places they have learned to come when called, poking their heads out of the water or climbing on the bank to be fed.

Americans may not consider the soft-shell turtle as sacred, but many do consider them almost as delicious to eat as the diamond-back terrapin. They are caught in traps and even on hook and line. Turtle fishermen bait their hooks with worms, bits of old meat, and sometimes with watermelon rind. For some strange reason, soft-shell turtles love watermelon rind.

Like the diamondback, soft-shells are sometimes raised on turtle farms and sold to restaurants for high prices.

53

5. Snapping Turtles

In a college class in zoology the professor was dissecting a snapping turtle. First he cut off its head. Then he reached for the body, intending to remove it from the shell. But his hand came close to the severed head. And it bit him.

At least that's the story, and it may have been true. The snapping turtle got its name honestly. The common snapper, *Chelydra serpentina*, will not only defend itself when annoyed, it will often advance and attack out of pure meanness. It has a big head, powerful jaws, a slightly hawk-shaped and razor-edged beak. All this is on the end of a long neck that the snapper can dart forward or sideways with the speed of a snake. It can even strike backward almost half the length of the shell.

Like the soft-shell, once the snapper bites, it is inclined to hold on. There have actually been cases where the beak of a snapping turtle kept its grip on a man's hand after its head had been completely cut from its body. The jaws of the dead turtle had to be pried open.

Fortunately the snapper, unlike the soft-shell, has a long tail. It can safely be picked up by the tail—as long as it is held far away from your body. However, a large snapper may be injured internally if handled this way.

Despite its foul temper on land, the snapper rarely tries to defend itself underwater. Here it merely retires into its shell.

There are two species of snappers: the giant alligator snapper, which we'll get to next, and *Chelydra serpentina*, usually called

The common snapping turtle is just as ugly tempered as it looks.

the common, or just *the* snapper. Fully grown, it has a carapace about twelve or fourteen inches long and weighs between twenty-five and forty pounds. It is found over most of the United States east of the Rockies and south into Central America. Actually it is far more numerous than it seems to be. Spending most of its time in the water, often in dark, muddy water, it is seldom seen.

The snapper's carapace is a sort of dirty brown, but with adults it is usually covered by algae. Even at the edge of a stream where it can be seen, the snapper looks more like a lump of grass or old wood than an animal. Here, motionless, it may wait until some unsuspecting fish or frog comes close. Then it strikes. Snappers also may swim underwater to catch a duck on the surface, drag it to the bottom, and tear it apart with its beak and claws.

The snapper's plastron is a dull yellow. It is cross-shaped and very small for the size of the turtle. This does not give it as much protection as some turtles have, but the large leg openings make it far more mobile than most. An excellent swimmer, the snapper can also move with surprising speed on land. In fact, it can actually jump, and sometimes does, to catch frogs, beetles, and other food.

About the only good thing—from a people's point of view—that can be said for the snapper is that it makes excellent food. Strangely, though turtle soup and meat are very popular in some parts of the country, they are almost unknown in others.

THE BEAST OF BUSCO

One spring morning in 1948, Mr. Gale Harris, a farmer who lived near Churubusco, Indiana, was standing on the roof of his barn. Looking across a nearby lake he saw, as he later told newspaper reporters, what he thought was a submarine: a huge, dark shadow just below the surface with a snorkel-like affair at one end. After a few moments of awed wonder Harris realized it was a turtle. The turtle, he reported, was easily as big as a dining-room table.

When the story appeared in the newspapers, people from Churubusco and neighboring towns descended on Mr. Harris' farm. Some of them brought boats, guns, spears. Some of them saw, or said they saw, the turtle. But nobody managed to spear or shoot it.

"The Beast of Busco," the newspapers called it, and still bigger crowds rushed to see the spectacle. They trampled all over Mr. Harris' farm, ruining his crops. In desperation he decided to drain the lake. But it was on fairly high ground. Water rushing out of the drainage ditch almost drowned two men working in a field downhill. Also, the lake turned out to be deeper than Harris had thought. It refused to empty, and quickly refilled.

For two summers "The Beast of Busco" made newspaper headlines. But gradually fewer and fewer persons came to look. With the end of the second summer "The Beast of Busco" disappeared from the news.

Undoubtedly the turtle Mr. Harris saw was an alligator snapper. Also, undoubtedly, it was not as big as some people thought. On the other hand, the alligator snapper, *Macrochelys temmincki*, can be the biggest of all freshwater turtles. Fully grown, one may have a thirty-inch carapace. Including the long neck and tail, it may be close to four feet and weigh around two hundred pounds. Down its back from one end to the other run three sharp ridges.

Happily, this monster is not quite as evil-tempered as its smaller cousin, the common snapper. It tends to lie placidly on the bottom, often in quite deep water, coming to the surface only now and then to breathe. On land it is not given to open attack as the other snapper may be. However, it can, and will, strike with blinding swiftness if bothered. Many persons claim that a grown alligator snapper could remove a man's hand with one bite or cut a broom handle in two. Ross Allen, the famed herpetologist of Silver Springs, Florida, says this is an exaggeration. When Allen nudged one of his grown alligator snappers with a new broom handle, it put a deep dent in the handle, but did not break it.

To capture alligator snappers for his animal farm, Mr. Allen

A small alligator snapper, but just as ugly as a big one.

swims along the bottom of likely streams and ponds. Like the common snapper, the carapace of the alligator snapper is covered with algae, making it very difficult to see. When Allen does find one, he carefully ties a line to its tail. Like the common snapper, the alligator snapper does not normally fight underwater. But pulled to the surface, it is something else. One bit a chunk out of a small boat in which Allen had placed it.

As a rule, alligator snappers are confined to that part of the country where the streams drain into the Gulf of Mexico. In the winter, where the weather is cold, both the alligator and common snapper dig into the muddy bottom of a lake or stream and hibernate. This probably explains the autumn disappearance of "The Beast of Busco."

Although it can be vicious out of the water, the alligator snapper is basically lazy. And the most curious thing about it is its manner of catching fish for food.

Growing on the tongue of the alligator snapper is a wormlike bit of flesh. It is fastened in the middle, and the snapper can wiggle either or both ends. Hungry, the big turtle merely settles down to the bottom of its pond or stream. With both its head and carapace covered by algae, it looks like part of the bottom. Even the eyes are almost hidden by the loose, wrinkled flesh around them. The turtle open its mouth, and waits. The little bit of flesh on its tongue wiggles exactly like a worm. When a passing fish swims close looking for a meal of its own—the big jaws slam shut. The turtle has its dinner.

6. Small Freshwater Turtles

Most of the turtles that spend their time in or near fresh water are smaller than the big snappers and soft-shells. Like all turtles, they must come on land to lay their eggs. With a few exceptions they do this singly rather than in *arribadas*, and their eggs are smaller, with more brittle shells, and fewer in number than those of the sea turtles.

One of the most common of the freshwater turtles in the eastern United States is the musk turtle, better known as stinkpot, stinking jim, or stinking jinny. Even the scientists call it *Sternotherus odoratus*, and the *odoratus* part fits it perfectly. Picked up roughly, it lets go with an odor that makes most creatures put it down again, in a hurry. This comes from a pair of glands in the soft skin just in front of the turtle's hind legs. If its smell is not defense enough, the stinkpot may also take a nip from a finger when provoked. But never more than four or five inches long, it can't do serious damage.

Although plentiful, the musk turtle is rarely seen. It spends much of its time lying on the bottom of its pond. Or it may float just below the surface with only the tip of its nose above water. When it does come ashore its dark shell is usually covered with moss, or mud, or both. The only pretty thing about it are two yellow stripes on each side of the head, one just over and one just under the eye.

The mud turtle, *Kinosternon subrubrum*, looks much like the musk turtle. It even smells like it, though maybe not quite as

The musk turtle, Sternotherus odoratus, *only rarely leaves the water to
sun itself.*

These turtles, Pseudemys scripta scripta, *are called "cooters," "yellow-
bellies," and "sliders" and various other names in different parts of the
country. If you see a half dozen or more turtles sunning themselves on a
rock or limb close to the water, they are quite likely to be yellow-bellied
turtles or one of its close relatives.*

The red-eared turtle, Pseudemys scripta elegans, *was once sold by the millions in pet shops. The name red-ear comes from a red or orange stripe behind the eye on most, but not all. This is an adult male, about seven inches long. Only males have the long fingernails.*

much. Like the musk turtle, it spends most of its time in the water. When it comes on land to lay its eggs, it wastes little time. Frequently it doesn't even dig a nest. Instead, it drops a couple of eggs in some crack in the ground, then goes on about its business. The babies, when hatched, are less than an inch long. But somehow they find their way back to the water, already hungry for fish eggs or whatever they can find small enough to swallow.

For boys who like to find and keep pet turtles, the spotted turtle, *Clemmys guttata*, is a big favorite. Only three to five inches long, its blackish shell has bright yellow or orange dots all over it. This turtle can be found in swamps and ponds over most of the eastern United States. It can often be seen on a rock or tree limb overhanging the water. Captured, it never bites and is easy to feed with snails, worms, and tiny bits of meat.

When it climbs out of the water to sun itself, the spotted turtle is generally alone. If you see a half dozen or more turtles on the same tree limb they are usually called sliders. Or they may be called cooters, or yellow bellies, or some other name, depending on the part of the country. Scientists call them *Pseudemys scripta* and then add still another name for the various sub-species. Baby *Pseudemys scripta elegans,* called red-eared turtles, were once sold by the millions in pet shops. Only an inch or so long, with a bright red or yellow stripe behind each ear, they looked very pretty in small aquariums. But strange as it may seem, keeping a pet turtle is not always as safe as it may appear. As a result, many areas now have laws against the sale of baby turtles.

7. Side-Necked Turtles

There are about fifty species of Pleurodira—the side-necked turtles. These don't draw their heads straight back into the shells. Instead, the neck is bent to the side until the head is hidden under the shell's edge. All the side-necked turtles live in the tropics in South America, Africa, Australia. Not very much is known about them. But at least two species are very odd and interesting.

One morning in 1799, a young German explorer named Alexander von Humboldt and French naturalist, Aimé Bonpland, were paddling a canoe up the Orinoco River in South America. They came to a low, flat island that was crowded with Indians. Men and boys dug in the sand to uncover thousands of round, white objects that the women carried away in baskets.

Neither von Humboldt or Bonpland had seen anything like it. They went ashore to watch. Luckily, there was a Spanish priest with the Indians, who explained what was happening.

Every year, the priest said, a kind of turtle called arrau came ashore to nest on islands in the river. The turtles did not always choose the same islands, but they did always choose low, flat ones. They came at night, by the thousands. So great was the number, the turtles crawled over one another to lay their eggs. Then they went back into the river.

Except at egg-laying time, the arrau did not normally live close together. Nor did they live in the river where they nested. Instead, they lived in ponds and lakes nearby. And though they spent much time in the water, their main food was fruit fallen from nearby trees.

The turtle eggs, the priest said, were an important part of the Indians' diet. More important, the eggs were made into what he called "turtle butter." This was actually an oil, much like olive oil. The Indians used it for cooking and to burn in lamps. Great quantities were sold to merchants who took the oil back to cities along the coast.

In amazement, von Humboldt asked how many eggs the Indians might gather in one season. It took five thousand eggs to fill one big earthen jar with oil, the priest said. And each year the two or three tribes with which he lived, filled about five thousand jars. That would be 25 million eggs, for these Indians alone.

To von Humboldt and Bonpland this seemed impossible. But a half century later an English naturalist on the Amazon River would estimate that the Indians in that area collected some 48 million eggs a year.

It is now known that the arrau, *Podocnemis expansa*, lives only along the Amazon and Orinoco river systems. It is one of the biggest of freshwater turtles. The female is always much bigger than the male, and she may have a carapace almost three feet in length.

The arrau is no longer as numerous as it once was. The tremendous number of eggs taken for commercial use threatened to destroy it, as the American buffalo was once destroyed. In time, however, other products replaced "turtle butter" for light and cooking in the coastal cities. Indians still gather the eggs for food, but the arrau now seems to be holding its own.

Probably the strangest of all turtles, at least as far as looks, is the matamata, *Chelys fimbriata*. This doesn't look like a turtle at all; in fact, it doesn't look like any living thing. One naturalist said it looked like a pile of wet leaves, which is a good description.

64

The shell of a female arrau turtle, Podocnemis expansa, *from the Amazon-Orinoco river valleys of South America. The males of this species are surprisingly rare, and much smaller than the female.*

The matamata lives along the muddy, slow-moving streams of northeastern South America. It may get to be eighteen inches long, but is usually smaller. The shell is covered with what looks like warts of various shapes, with moss growing between them. The skinny neck is almost as long as the shell. The head and legs are covered with wrinkled skin that hangs in tassels. These sway with the slow-moving water. On the front of the head is a long, snorkel-like snout. The whole thing is about as ugly as a living creature can be. When the Indians in northeast Brazil refer to someone as *cara de matamata*—meaning he has the face of a matamata—it is not meant to be a compliment.

Even so, the matamata's looks are perfectly fitted to its manner of feeding. Lazy, slow-moving—except for the neck and mouth

65

This is a matamata, Chelys fimbriata, *probably the ugliest of all turtles. This one was raised in captivity and does not have the mass of algae growing on its back that it might have in the wild.*

—the turtle spends most of its time lying on the bottom in shallow water. The water gently moves the fringes of its skin. To a passing fish this may look like bits of food. The fish comes closer.

Now the matamata moves. The long neck shoots forward. The mouth opens wide. And what a mouth! For the size of the turtle, it's tremendous. When it opens, water rushes in, carrying the fish with it. The matamata spits out the water, swallows the fish, and goes back to waiting.

8. Land Turtles, Large and Small

As mentioned earlier, land turtles are often called tortoises. There are about forty species, and one or another may be found over most of the tropic and temperate world. They have hard shells and with few exceptions can retract their heads all the way inside. Their legs are made more for digging than swimming. Heavily scaled, they are often shaped like those of a miniature elephant. The claws are long and sharp.

Although practically all turtles can swim if they have to, some tortoises never do. Instead, the gopher tortoise of the United States prefers dry, sandy, and sometimes actually desert country.

There are several species of gopher turtles, without much difference between them. Probably the most common, *Gopherus polyphemus*, (most people just call it a gopher) is found from South Carolina to Texas. For a home it digs a tunnel that may be forty feet long and ten feet deep. These spacious living quarters are often shared, willingly or unwillingly, with other animals. Insects of various kinds move into a gopher hole. Lizards and a small frog called a gopher frog set up housekeeping there to eat the insects. The gopher turtle eats some of the insects itself, but its main diet is plants. Its relations with the lizards and frogs seem to be friendly.

Sometimes snakes, particularly rattlers, move into a gopher

The common gopher makes his home in dry, sandy country. Here he is feeding on prickly pear cactus, unbothered by the thorns.

A baby gopher turtle, but already with claws for digging.

hole. Apparently the snakes and the gophers get along together. However, people have seen a gopher prevent a rattlesnake's entrance by blocking the hole with its body. The gopher was head down in the hole, its legs pulled tight in its shell. This presented the snake with nothing but a solid block of shell and no way to get past.

The desert tortoise, *Gopherus agassizi,* is found from southern Nevada to Mexico, feeding mainly on cactus. From this, oddly enough, it can get a rather large amount of pure water, and can store this in its bladder for future use.

Of all turtles, the box turtle, *Terrapene carolina,* has the tightest fitting suit of armor. It can do more than pull its head and legs completely underneath the carapace. The plastron has a hinge near the middle so that both its front and back are movable. The box turtle can close these so tightly it's impossible to slip a blade of grass between the upper and lower shell. Although only five or six inches long, this turtle is safe against practically all enemies. If a dog or some other animal grabs one, the turtle merely closes its shell and waits. After a while the dog gets tired of chewing on what must feel like a rock and puts it down. The turtle then goes about its own business.

The main business of the box turtle is eating: grass, fruit, insects, worms. In fact, given enough blackberries or fruit, the box turtle will almost eat itself out of its own shell. It will get so fat that when its head and neck are pulled all the way underneath the carapace, the back legs are pushed out.

Box turtles—there are several species—are found throughout the eastern half of the United States. All have a humpbacked carapace, with the front and back edges curled slightly upward. The basic color is brown, and across this run either stripes or broad splotches of yellow or orange. Normally a creature of dry woods and fields, now and then a box turtle will waddle into shallow water at the edge of a pond and soak itself for hours.

This is the little box turtle that can close its shell so tightly not even an ant could crawl in.

The box turtle has, perhaps, the most placid disposition of any turtle. Picked up, it merely withdraws into its shell and stays there until it is put down again.

Possibly the most world famous of all turtles are the giant tortoises of the Galápagos Islands. When Spanish explorers first discovered these uninhabited islands in the sixteenth century they were amazed at the number and size of the tortoises. Weighing up to six hundred pounds and more, they seemed to be everywhere. Slow, placid, they were easy to capture.

At this time sailors on long voyages often became diseased and died because of poor diet. The turtles offered excellent fresh meat. Loaded on the ships, upside down and helpless on their backs, they would still live for months. So the whaling ships, the pirates, the men-of-war, every ship that came to the Galápagos Islands carried away all the turtles it could hold. It is estimated

70

that between 200,000 and 300,000 turtles were killed in this way during the eighteenth and nineteenth centuries.

Even worse for the turtles, rats escaped from some of the ships, and pigs were released on the islands. The pigs and rats multiplied. They ate the turtle eggs and baby turtles. At the same time, visitors were slaughtering and taking away the adults. Gradually the turtles disappeared from some of the islands. On other islands only a few remained, hidden in the mountainous interior where they were hard to find. Actually, the species varied slightly from one island to another, though all were very much alike.

Eventually the government of Ecuador, which owns the Galápagos Islands, passed laws protecting the turtles. Scientific expeditions were sent to study them.

Two naturalists who have studied these tortoises are Craig and Jan MacFarland, who took along their baby daughter Bennett. For months the MacFarlands moved from one island to another, living in tents close to the tortoises' nesting grounds.

This is a Galápagos turtle, Geochelone elephantopus hoodenis, *from Hood Island in the Galápagos.*

They found the giants so placid that often they used one's back as a comfortable place to change Bennett's diapers.

On the other hand, these tortoises could be as destructive as a bulldozer. Once one decided it was easier to crawl through the MacFarland's tent than to go around it. So it did, ripping the tent, overturning cots, and smashing a five-gallon water can. It also ate a pair of Craig's socks on the way. Normally, however, these tortoises eat whatever plants are available, including cactus.

The females lay their eggs twice a year, usually in the same place. There may be anywhere from two to seventeen eggs, about ten on the average. Using her hind feet, the female carefully spreads them into a single layer. Then she spreads dirt over them, packing it down with her body. Depending on the weather, it takes from three to eight months for the eggs to hatch. At birth the young weigh about three ounces—a long way from the three hundred to six hundred pounds they will weigh later.

9. Turtles and Men, and the Turtles' Future

When Christopher Columbus discovered what he thought was India, he found the Indians eating sea turtles. The turtles helped Columbus' sailors, and many of the early explorers who followed, stay alive and healthy. They played an important role in the exploration of the New World.

Today turtles are still an important part in the diet of many persons in South and Central America, the West Indies, parts of Australia, and other places. No one can blame a hungry person for eating what he needs. But the world's population is increasing rapidly. Men have learned to destroy turtles faster than the turtles can reproduce. It's like the old story of the farmer and his corn: if he eats it all one winter, there's none left for planting. Today many species of turtles are in danger of being wiped out.

The sea turtles are the most important for food, and are the most endangered. In 1967, turtle hunters in Mexico took 10,540 tons of turtles, along with a vast but uncounted number of eggs, from the beaches. Most of these were sold to persons who were not hungry but believed that turtle meat would help their sex life.

Many nesting beaches, once uninhabited by human beings, are now lined with houses. On some of the South and Central American beaches the natives use pigs to hunt the turtle eggs. The pigs, kept on leashes, smell the eggs, root them up, and the men take them. The turtles themselves are turned on their backs, then taken away by the shipload. In the sea the turtles are caught in giant nets or speared.

In Europe and the United States the automobile is a major killer of land turtles. Fifteen or twenty years ago their crushed bodies littered the highways. Today relatively few are seen, because so many have been destroyed.

There is another angle to the story. Only a few years ago approximately 13 million small, freshwater turtles were raised on turtle farms and sold as pets each year. Almost everyone who had an aquarium, even if it only held two goldfish, also had a turtle. But the dry pet food given the goldfish did not make a proper diet for the turtles. They became sick. A lack of sunlight softened their shells, caused fungus, and the turtles died.

Then doctors learned that pet turtles could kill as well as be

These were the living quarters of Dr. Pritchard and other herpetologists studying turtles on the beach in Surinam in South America.

On a beach in Central America, government workers rebury eggs of the green turtle, Chelonia mydas. *Taken from beaches where they were in danger of being destroyed by other animals, these are reburied in protected places.*

killed. Raised in crowded and polluted tanks, many of them carried germs on their backs. Called salmonella bacteria, these germs particularly affected small children. If the child touched his pet turtle, then put his fingers in his mouth or handled food, he might become seriously ill or even die. Many places now have laws against the sale of these small turtles.

Even so, a turtle in a garden or yard where it can roam at will can become an interesting pet. And the best way to know the turtle is healthy is to find one in the wild, in its native home.

Despite the decreasing number of turtles around the world, there is some hope for their future. Many countries have passed laws protecting the nesting beaches of the great sea turtles.

Naturalists like Dr. Archie Carr and Peter Pritchard have spent years studying turtles and learning to protect them. In their work they have carried literally thousands of eggs from endangered beaches to new and better places. Here the eggs are hatched, the baby turtles kept in ponds until they are big enough to be safe from most dangers. Then they are released into the sea. It is hoped that five or six years later the mature turtles will return to these same beaches to breed. In this way new nesting beaches may be established. So far, however, no one knows if this will work. And the most recent results are discouraging.

In the West Indies, Australia, and other places, turtle farms are trying to raise giant sea turtles. It is still too early to know just how successful they will be.

For many persons in various parts of the world the turtle is still an important source of food. To them its total destruction would be a true tragedy. But the saving of turtles, all species of turtles, is important to many persons who will never use them for food. It is a happy sight to watch a small box turtle eating its slow way across a grassy field. And anyone who has seen a giant leatherback swimming in the open ocean will never forget the sight.

Man has it in his power now to destroy all species of turtles. Or he can save them—if people care enough.

Index

ABOUT THE AUTHOR

WYATT BLASSINGAME was born and brought up in Alabama. He graduated from the University of Alabama and did graduate work in English there, at the University of Florida, and at New York University. Except for one year on a newspaper, three years in the United States Navy during World War II, and some part-time teaching, he has been a professional writer all his life.

Mr. Blassingame has had more than six hundred stories and articles published in magazines, anthologies, and textbooks, here and abroad. He has written four adult novels and more than thirty books for young readers.

He is the author of two other popular books in this series of nature books, WONDERS OF ALLIGATORS AND CROCODILES and WONDERS OF FROGS AND TOADS.

Mr. Blassingame lives in Anna Maria, Florida.